THE BBC
Book of Dinosaurs

Paul Appleby

Illustrated by Gill Tomblin

BBC BOOKS

Published by BBC Books,
a division of BBC Enterprises Limited,
Woodlands, 80 Wood Lane, London W12 OTT
First Published 1990
© Paul Appleby 1990
ISBN 0 563 36055 0

Designed by Martin Bronkhorst
Illustrations © Gill Tomblin 1990

Set in Century Expanded
Printed in Great Britain by Cambus Litho Ltd,
East Kilbride
Colour separations by Dot Gradations Ltd, Chelmsford

To Liz

Contents

What is a Dinosaur?

This is a detective story. It starts with the remains of several dead bodies, but instead of trying to find a murderer, we're investigating the lives of the victims – the animals called dinosaurs!

The bodies have been fossilised. Over millions of years, the bone has been replaced by hard rock and all the soft parts have vanished. All that's left from millions of animals are individual bones, a few complete skeletons, some tiny fragments of fossil skin and some eggs!

It's patchy evidence, but the bones immediately tell us the size and shape of the animal and, with a great deal of skill, it's possible to piece together the fossil bones and re-build the dinosaur skeleton.

But that's just a tiny part of the story, because dinosaurs were animals – living, breathing, snorting, smelly reptiles; and that's what we're interested in – bringing dinosaurs back to life.

What did they eat? How fast could they run? Did they live in herds? To find out we will use the fossil evidence and look at animals that are alive now. With a little imagination, we can turn the bones into real animals.

What is a dinosaur? It's a reptile, with a tough scaly skin, legs that end in claws, and a long tail, just like many reptiles alive today. But unlike any modern reptile, dinosaurs stood with their legs underneath their body, rather than sprawling out to the sides. That sounds a minor detail, but it made dinosaur movement very efficient, allowing some dinosaurs to stand on their hind legs and develop hands, whilst others grew to a huge size!

Iguanodon did both: it was a 10-metre-long reptile, three times taller than a man, that could stand on its hind legs!

Iguanodon's fingers end in small hooves, so it sometimes walked on all fours. The thumb is a spike, possibly a weapon.

An *Iguanodon* skeleton, standing on all fours. The bones show the outline of the animal, and there are marks where muscles were attached, so the skeleton can be "fleshed out" and a real animal starts to take shape! The skull, with plant-crushing teeth at the back of the jaw, and a horny beak at the front, tells us what it ate. And the muscle scars on the hind legs show *Iguanodon* could stand upright to reach the best leaves or look out for predators, with its tail acting as a counter-balance.

Modern reptiles have no eyelids or earlobes, so the same was probably true for dinosaurs!

Reptiles have a tough scaly skin, which they shed when they grow.

Imagine a herd of 10-metre Iguanodons browsing through a swampy woodland, 120 million years ago, occasionally grunting to their young, or stopping to stand and sniff the air. The plant-eating Green Iguana (right) is the modern equivalent. Its skin, mouth and eyes are all similar, but it's 50 times smaller.

Most reptiles have a long tail – very useful for balancing!

No modern reptiles have straight legs like the dinosaurs – only mammals and birds can stand like this!

The Age of the Dinosaurs

Dinosaurs were very important animals. They completely dominated the Earth for over 100 million years! Such an awesome figure can only begin to make sense when you look at the whole history of Planet Earth and, once again, it's rocks and fossils that provide the evidence.

It's thought that the planet formed from dust and gas about 4500 million years ago (mya), and even now the outer crust moves round on a core of molten rock, which sometimes breaks through to cause volcanoes.

Early chemical reactions formed water, which lay on the surface as seas, while the atmosphere was a mixture of poisonous gases. For the first half of the Earth's history, there was no life. It was not until 2000 million years ago that the first microscopic plants appeared.

Animals eat plants, so they could only evolve once there was enough plant life to support them. Similarly, carnivores evolved after herbivores, so the path to the Age of Dinosaurs has a number of simple steps:

225 mya: The Triassic Period, the start of the Dinosaur Age. One huge land mass, Pangaea, covers most of the northern hemisphere, creating stable, warm weather, even near the Poles. There are two types of dinosaur, with different hip arrangements; "ornithischians", with bird-like hips, and "saurischians", with reptile-like hips. Dinosaurs vary in size, but already many are bigger than a man.

TRIASSIC

CRETACEOUS

135 mya: The Cretaceous period. The continents are separated, but their shapes are very different from those of today. Herds of hadrosaurs and ceratopsids roam the open plains, under threat from tyrannosaurs. More importantly, the first flowers develop!

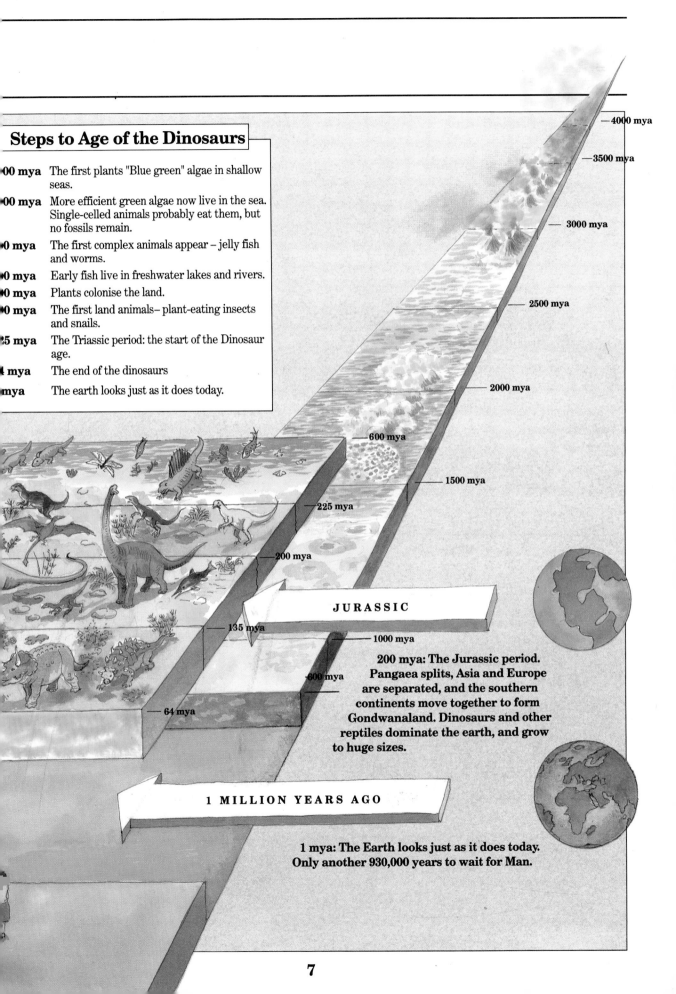

Steps to Age of the Dinosaurs

·00 mya	The first plants "Blue green" algae in shallow seas.
·00 mya	More efficient green algae now live in the sea. Single-celled animals probably eat them, but no fossils remain.
·0 mya	The first complex animals appear – jelly fish and worms.
·0 mya	Early fish live in freshwater lakes and rivers.
·0 mya	Plants colonise the land.
·0 mya	The first land animals– plant-eating insects and snails.
·5 mya	The Triassic period: the start of the Dinosaur age.
·4 mya	The end of the dinosaurs
·mya	The earth looks just as it does today.

4000 mya

3500 mya

3000 mya

2500 mya

2000 mya

600 mya

1500 mya

225 mya

200 mya

JURASSIC

135 mya

1000 mya

·600 mya

64 mya

200 mya: The Jurassic period. Pangaea splits, Asia and Europe are separated, and the southern continents move together to form Gondwanaland. Dinosaurs and other reptiles dominate the earth, and grow to huge sizes.

1 MILLION YEARS AGO

1 mya: The Earth looks just as it does today. Only another 930,000 years to wait for Man.

The Rise of the Dinosaurs

How did the dinosaurs come to rule the Earth? The story starts with freshwater fish, 300 million years before the Age of the Dinosaurs.

500 million years ago, fish were the most complex animals on Earth, and the first animals to have a backbone.

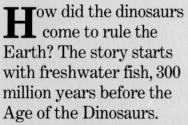

2 Amphibians

The first true amphibians date fro[m] about 340 mya. The [most] famous fossil is called *Ichthyostega*, a 90 cm animal very similar t[o] this salamander.

While lungfish crawl around on their fin[s], amphibians walk on jointe[d] legs with 5 toes. Their vision and hearing are adapted for the a[ir] but they still need water for the e[gg] and tadpole stages, and their thin skin dries out quickly in air unles[s it] is kept moist. So the[y] can't venture f[ar] onto land.

1 Lungfish

Fish are adapted for life in water, with a strong tail, a streamlined body, and gills for taking oxygen from the water, rather than lungs like ours.

But some fish can live on land! Lungfish like this are found in Africa today, using their lungs to survive when their lakes dry out. Ancient lungfish also came onto land to eat insects and land plants, and avoid predators.

As each generation of lungfish spent more time on land, their fins became stronger, and better for walking on, until the fish were able to live in water or on land.

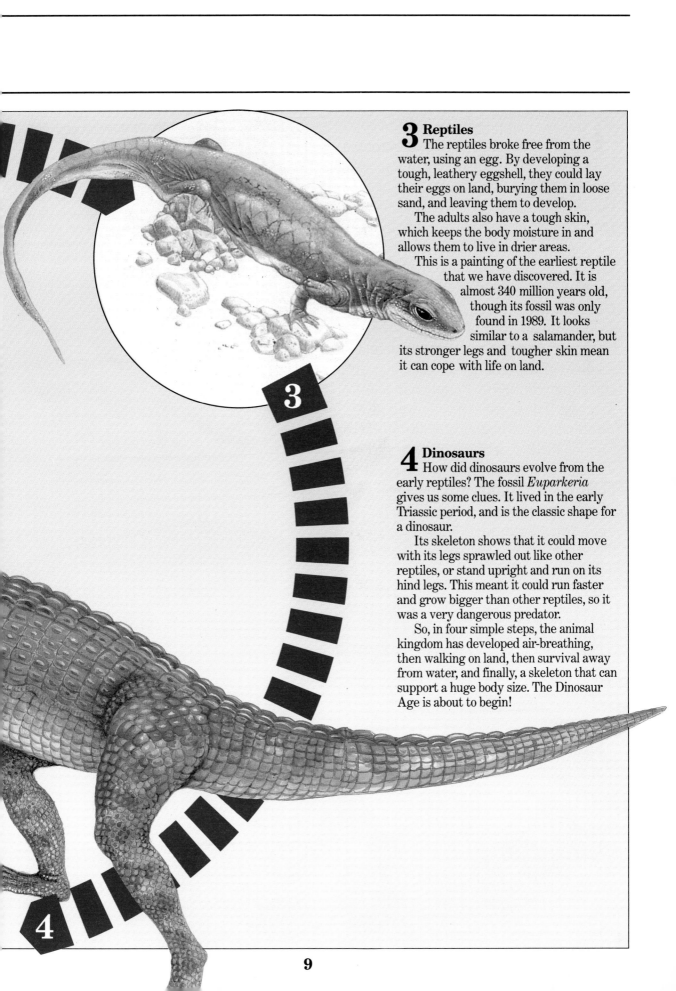

3 Reptiles

The reptiles broke free from the water, using an egg. By developing a tough, leathery eggshell, they could lay their eggs on land, burying them in loose sand, and leaving them to develop.

The adults also have a tough skin, which keeps the body moisture in and allows them to live in drier areas.

This is a painting of the earliest reptile that we have discovered. It is almost 340 million years old, though its fossil was only found in 1989. It looks similar to a salamander, but its stronger legs and tougher skin mean it can cope with life on land.

4 Dinosaurs

How did dinosaurs evolve from the early reptiles? The fossil *Euparkeria* gives us some clues. It lived in the early Triassic period, and is the classic shape for a dinosaur.

Its skeleton shows that it could move with its legs sprawled out like other reptiles, or stand upright and run on its hind legs. This meant it could run faster and grow bigger than other reptiles, so it was a very dangerous predator.

So, in four simple steps, the animal kingdom has developed air-breathing, then walking on land, then survival away from water, and finally, a skeleton that can support a huge body size. The Dinosaur Age is about to begin!

What was the First Dinosaur?

This is an impossible question to answer, because the fossil remains only cover a fraction of the living dinosaurs, and new discoveries are being made all the time! The earliest fossils date from the later Triassic period, about 215 million years ago, and include a number of types – *Herrarasaurus*, *Staurikosaurus*, and the best known of the early dinosaurs, *Coelophysis*.

A large number of *Coelophysis* skeletons have been discovered, including a whole group that lived on the coast of the super-continent Pangaea in the Triassic. These were discovered as a jumbled pile of bodies at a site in New Mexico in 1947, and it's likely that they were swept down-river to the coast by a flood, over 200 million years ago.

Coelophysis was a classic early dinosaur, a light, long-legged bipedal reptile, and like nothing on earth today!

Imagine a *Coelophysis*, loping along on all fours, when suddenly it sees a victim, just ahead. It jumps u on its hind legs and breaks into a run, its arms reaching forwards, its tail streaming behind like a rudder. It runs down the lizard and kills it in a cloud of dust...

It probably ran like this roadrunner, (below) a reptile-eating bird from the Arizona desert. Although they can fly, roadrunners hunt on the ground, and can do 40 kph in short bursts, using their feathered tail for balance. But they are just a quarter the size of *Coelophysis*.

An adult *Coelophysis* (above) was quite big – over 3 metres from head to tail. It's legs and toes were long, so it could run quite fast, and the leg shape shows that it could have walked on all fours or stood upright to a height of 1.5 metres. By walking upright it could use its forelimbs as 'arms'. Its claws could be used for pinning down prey, but not for picking it up, so it probably ripped its food just like a bird of prey.

We know that it ate meat – insects, reptiles and amphibians – because it had sharp, serrated teeth, not the peg-like teeth of a plant-eater.

Plateosaurus

Coelophysis

Lesothosaurus

Coelophysis was just one type of Triassic dinosaur, since already there were several distinct groups. It was a "theropod", a group of agile carnivorous dinosaurs that eventually gave rise to the birds and tyrannosaurs.

Plateosaurus **was the first** really big dinosaur, up to 8 metres long. It was the first "sauropod", a group that expanded in the Jurassic period to include all the biggest dinosaurs. It had the classic sauropod shape – a bulky body and a long neck and tail – but was just one-tenth of the size of the later sauropods! *Plateosaurus* was a plant-eater, with clawed, grasping feet.

Lesothosaurus **was an early** "ornithischian" dinosaur, with a light body and long legs like *Coelophysis*, but only 90 cm long. The ornithischians were all plant-eaters, and eventually included *Iguanodon* and the hadrosaurs, as animals like *Triceratops*, you can see on the next page.

Dinosaur Evolution

The "saurischian" group includes all the major carnivores. The big ones slowly

got bigger, as *Allosaurus* gave way to *Tyrannosaurus*, and the small ones became more dangerous

and faster, as *Ornithol* was replaced by *Deinony* and *Struthiomimus*.

The sauropods were numerous in the Jurassic

period, but had almost died out by the Cretaceous

The "ornithischian" dinosaurs were plant-eaters, both four-legged and bipedal.

The later species were more specialised feeders, eating the flowering plants, which appeared in

the Cretaceous and had bet defences against the saurisch carnivores.

These two pages cover 140 million years, and feature some of the world's most famous animals – ones that no human has ever seen! Dinosaurs cover a huge range of size, shape, speed, feeding habits and time, yet they're often lumped together.

There were over 5 million generations of dinosaurs, and each generation was more suited to its habitat, so there were major changes throughout the Dinosaur Age. By looking at fossil bones we can group species together, but it's impossible to say that one species was directly descended from another. However, we can see some definite trends in dinosaur biology.

The man-sized Triassic dinosaurs gave rise to huge animals in the Jurassic, including the largest sauropods and carnivores like *Allosaurus*. But both these types were extinct well before the end of the Dinosaur Age, with only a few obscure sauropods surviving. The fastest, most dangerous, best armoured and cleverest dinosaurs appeared in the Cretaceous period, the climax of dinosaur evolution.

What was the Smallest Dinosau

Dinosaurs were generally big animals. The vast majority were bigger than an adult human, and much bigger than modern reptiles. But the dinosaurs covered a huge range with *Compsognathus* amongst the smallest. *Compsognathus* was about 70 cm long, but that was mostly tail, and it weighed just a few kilograms – one fifty-thousandth of the weight of the *Brachiosaurus* on the next page. Even so, it was a lot bigger than many modern lizards!

Compsognathus was a coelurosaur like *Coelophysis*, but it lived much later, in the Jurassic period about 140 million years ago. Being small, it had a limited food supply, and its light skull and spiky teeth mean it probably ate small animal prey such as insects or small lizards.

Its long tail and hind legs show that it walked bipedally, and it ran on three long toes, with the first toe reduced to a claw further up the leg, a pattern that is quite common in fast-running animals. The fore limbs are much shorter than the hind legs and have two claws for holding down prey.

Compsognathus would have needed its speed not just to catch prey, but to avoid larger predators. Even so, it probably had a short life span, and may have laid large clutches of eggs to ensure the survival of the species.

Compsognathus

A warm-blooded Reptile?

Modern reptiles are cold-blooded, taking their body temperature from the air around them like this sand lizard (left) basking in the the sun, rather than generating their own warmth just as birds and mammals do.

There have always been arguments about whether dinosaurs were warm-blooded, or cold-blooded like modern reptiles. Many biologists believe that dinosaurs had to be warm-blooded in order to be as active as their skeletons suggest they were. But warm-blooded animals need a lot more food than cold-blooded ones, in order to generate their own body heat.

Huge dinosaurs would probably have been able to stay warm quite easily, but small dinosaurs like *Compsognathus* would have faced a real problem finding enough food for the luxury of warm-bloodedness. It's very difficult to decide one way or the other, because the fossil bones can't give us any clues.

This is how the body

of a *Compsognathus* appears as a fossil (left), with its neck bent back by the contraction of the neck ligaments after it died.

Small fossils are only formed where the rock is fine enough to fill in the tiny bones, and all the *Compsognathus* specimens that have been found were in fine-grained lithographic limestone in Europe. It is possible that there were thousands of different types of small dinosaur, but we will never know because the chances of finding a specimen are so low!

This picture

shows *Compsognathus* next to the foot of an *Iguanodon*. *Iguanodon* was not the biggest dinosaur – but it was fourteen times bigger than *Compsognathus*.

What was the Biggest Dinosaur

If the problem with the smallest dinosaurs is finding a rock fine enough to preserve a tiny skeleton, the problem with the biggest dinosaurs is getting the bones out once you've found them! Huge individual bones have been found, but the largest complete skeleton is of *Brachiosaurus*, the current holder of the record as heaviest dinosaur.

Brachiosaurus was a sauropod dinosaur, a four-legged plant-eater. It was 22 metres long, stood 12 metres tall and weighed in at over 70 tonnes, ten times heavier than an African elephant.

The longest dinosaur was another sauropod, *Diplodocus*. It was 27 metres lo[ng] with a very long thin "whiplash" tail. It ha[d a] slender build in comparison to *Brachiosau[rus]* so it weighed a meagre 11 tonnes!

Both types appeared in the Jurassic pe[riod] having evolved from *Plateosaurus*. Anima[ls] were growing bigger to exploit the rich vegetation of the high tree-ferns and as a protection against predators. The adults would have been able to spot approaching danger from a long distance, and their she[er] weight and whiplash tail would be an effec[tive] deterrent against most predators.

The most extraordinary piece of sauropod engineering is the neck of the Chinese dinosaur *Mamenchisaurus*, which at 15 metres is almost three times longer than a giraffe's. It has 19 huge vertebrae, and would span three houses – the longest neck ever.

Diplodocus and _Brachiosaurus_ skeletons

- The leg bones are thick pillars, designed to support the weight.
- The ribs and some of the backbones are hollow to reduce weight without reducing strength.
- The neck is almost half the body length, requiring a special blood supply to pump blood up to the head.
- The head itself is tiny, no bigger than a horses's, with simple, peg-like teeth, and nostrils on the forehead. These were the biggest animals ever to walk the earth, but we still don't understand exactly how they managed it.

Waiting in the wings...

Since 1985, American scientists have been trying to excavate a huge fossil from incredibly hard rock in New Mexico. When the skeleton of _Seismosaurus_, a diplodocid, is finally assembled, it will probably stand over 40 metres long – the largest land animal ever.

Brachiosaurus

Diplodocus

How did the Big Dinosaurs Mov

The worst thing about only seeing dinosaurs as mounted skeletons in a museum is that they don't move! This is completely unnatural because every living animal moves – looking around, sniffing the wind, scratching, walking, trotting or even galloping. We've seen how the smaller, bipedal dinosaurs got around, and the larger carnivores would move in the same way, but how did the huge sauropods move?

The sauropods were very heavy, so their leg bones were solid pillars, kept straight under their body to support their weight. They had to keep two of their four feet on the ground at all times, so they could only walk, not trot or gallop. The same is true of elephants, but they manage to move quickly over short distances using a "quick march", just like speeded-up-walking. Maybe the sauropods did the same?

Fortunately, there's quite a lot of evidence to help our imagination, including footprints left by the dinosaurs themselves!

These are the fossilised footprints (right) of a Cretaceous hadrosaur) which was found in British Columbia. A trackway like this provides a lot of information. The individual prints show the size of the feet, and the weight on each foot, while the layout shows the length of the stride and the leg length, and the separation of the legs on each side of the body. The pattern of the prints will be different for a walking animal and a runner, though most prints have been left by walking animals, carefully skirting the soft ground that would have recorded their movement for posterity.

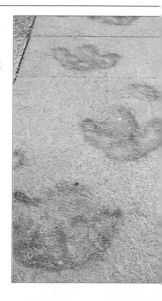

Apatosaurus

These elephants (right) have the same stiff-legged walking action as a sauropod dinosaur. The biggest sauropod, *Brachiosaurus*, had round feet with stubby toenails just like an elephant's, except that the *Brachiosaurus'* feet covered an area of 8000 square centimetres and supported an animal weighing 77 tonnes.

One of the best trackway fossils was found at Purgatory River in the USA, and it showed a herd of *Apatosaurus* with the smaller, younger animals in the centre of the group, surrounded by the much larger adults.

Apatosaurus was one of the largest sauropods, a bulky relative of *Diplodocus* over 20 metres long and weighing 30 tonnes. Many scientists now think that the tail was held clear of the ground, and even waved around like a whiplash – 3 metres long. If this is the case, all those museum skeletons with the tails dragging on the ground are completely wrong.

What did the Herbivores Eat?

Most dinosaurs were plant-eaters, but their food was very different from the grasses, bushes and trees that are around today. Plant fossils, in the form of seeds, leaves, and even whole trees, show that in the Jurassic period the main plants were tree ferns, and simple trees called ginkgos and cycads.

Cycads were like huge ferns with a thick woody trunk, but ginkgos are more like ordinary trees, with soft leaves.

These provided the food for the large dinosaurs like *Diplodocus*, and because all the best food leaves and young branches was high off the ground, they needed their long necks just to reach it.

There are still some dense areas of tree-ferns today, in the uplands of tropical islands where the climate is warm but wet, and the ferns can absorb moisture from the air. These ones are in the Mount Apo National Park in the Phillipines, but they also occur in New Zealand and grow over 30 metres tall in the New Hebrides.

Parasaurolophus

These are another type of simple plant that was a staple food of dinosaurs. Giant horsetails (right) once grew to 15 metres with rough spiky leaves, but once the climate dried out their lack of proper roots meant they could only survive as smaller species, living in damp areas, which is where they are found today.

All plant-eaters have to spend a lot of the day eating, but the huge *Diplodocus* (left) had a head no bigger than a horse's, with very simple peg-like teeth. How could it eat enough to survive? It probably wouldn't need as much food as a warm-blooded mammal, but even so the simple mouth must only have been for ripping up the vegetation. Getting the goodness out of leaves and twigs takes a lot more work.

Birds have the same problem, but solve the problem by eating stones, storing them in a muscular stomach called the gizzard, and grinding down tough seeds by mashing them up together. Smoothed-down stones have been found within the fossil skeleton of some dinosaurs, so they may have had a huge gizzard too.

In the mid-Cretaceous, everything started to change, as the flowering plants slowly replaced the ancient types. These plants had flowers like the magnolia (above), fruit and underground tubers in addition to leaves, providing much more food for the dinosaurs, much nearer the ground.

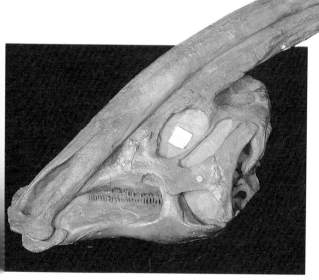

The new types of food took more chewing, so in the Cretaceous hadrosaurs, like this *Parasaurolophus*, the mouth is much more important in feeding.

At the front is a horny beak for snipping off fruit or twigs, and behind that a battery of densely-packed teeth, with ridges of enamel that fit together to squash the vegetation flat.

To make the tooth-batteries fit perfectly, the skull is very flexible, so when the hadrosaur bites, the upper jaw moves outwards. Modern mammals, such as camels, chew by moving the jaws sideways and pushing food into the cheeks and it is possible that hadrosaurs could do this too – but that's something that wouldn't show up in a fossil skull.

What did the Carnivores Eat?

The most famous dinosaurs are the huge meat-eaters, the biggest land carnivores ever! But did these huge monsters attack the big plant-eaters? Probably not – a hunter always looks for a small, old, weak or injured animals rather than risk an injury by taking on a large prey, especially one that can protect itself. And even if you could kill an animal the size of an *Apatosaurus*, just imagine how long it would take to eat it.

Carnivorous dinosaurs were well-armed with teeth and claws, but probably used their strength to kill and eat smaller dinosaurs, or other reptiles. They could also frighten smaller carnivores off their kills, since eating dead meat – carrion – is a lot safer and easier than killing your own food.

Allosaurus (above) was a classic carnivore, with over 70 pointed teeth curved backwards and with sharp, serrated edges. Its open skull was packed with the muscles attached to strong, biting jaws.

Ornitholestes (above) was a bipedal hunter from the Jurassic period, with long running-legs and very effective hands. It had two very long claws, and a shorter third claw which could be turned in to form a pincer, so *Ornitholestes* could pick up objects rather than just clawing at them. This is very rare amongst modern reptiles, but is more common in birds such as macaws.

It's thought that these smaller, agile dinosaurs preyed on mammals, and they became so successful that mammals became nocturnal burrowing animals just to keep out of their way. They certainly could not compete with the fast, dangerous and daytime predators like *Ornitholestes*.

Eggs are another easy source of good, nutritious food, and dinosaurs laid lots of them! Most were buried in the earth and left to develop, so a predator that could identify new nests would have an easy time feeding, without any danger of injury from its prey. *Oviraptor* was probably just such a dinosaur, a medium-sized bipedal carnivore, standing just over a metre tall, and with long, clawed hands, very useful for unearthing the eggs. It had a horny beak, with a deep lower jaw and a crest above the nose, giving it strong jaws which were ideal for breaking into tough dinosaur eggs and lapping up the contents.

One *Oviraptor* fossil was found on top of a clutch of *Protoceratop*s eggs in Mongolia – but it takes so long for bones to fossilise that we can't say it was caught stealing!

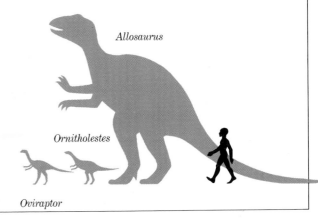

Allosaurus

Ornitholestes

Oviraptor

Reptiles Rule the World!

What animals do you see around you today? There are plenty of birds, the occasional frog or toad, and if you're lucky a mammal: a wild fox, rabbit or bat. It's very rare to see a wild reptile, yet in the Jurassic period reptiles were the most important animal group on Earth. Not only was there a huge range of dinosaurs, from *Compsognathus* to *Brachiosaurus*, but there were flying reptiles, and reptiles living in the seas!

The animals shown on these two pages were not dinosaurs but they were closely related, advanced reptiles unlike anything alive today. And they were wiped out by the same event as the dinosaurs.

Flying Reptiles

Over forty different types of pterosaur hav been discovered, the earliest dating from the Triassic period at the dawn of the dinosaur age. All have membrane wings supported by an enormous fourth finger, and they come in two main groups – rhamphorhyncoids and pterodactyloids.

Swimming Reptiles

The huge fish stocks in the shallow Jurassi seas led the reptiles to invade the water, changing legs and feet into flippers. The swimming reptiles formed three main groups – plesiosaurs, pliosaurs and ichthyosaurs. All three fed on fish.

In many ways, Rhamphorhyncoids were simple reptiles, keeping their long reptile tail, possibly for use as a rudder, and simple reptile teeth.

Rhamphorhyncus had a long skull with forward-pointing teeth at the front of the mouth, which it used to trap insects, flying with its mouth open and using it as a net in the air.

Pterodactyloids had a short tail, more like a bird's, and they grew much larger. The biggest species was the Cretaceous pterosaur *Quetzalcoatylus*, which had a wingspan of 11 metres – about the size of a small aeroplane!

Quetzalcoatylus

Rhamphorhyncus

Plesiosaurus

How did Pterosaurs fly?

The _Pteranodon_ skeleton is a brilliant flying design. The largest one was 7 metres across.
● It is compact, with a short tail and hollow bones, strengthened where there is most stress.
● The head has a long, toothless beak. The crest balances the beak without needing heavy muscles, and acts as a rudder.

Pteranodon

- The eyes are large, and the brain is very bird-like, with large centres for vision and balance, vital in flight.

- The wing is attached to the fourth finger, so a slight move of the finger would completely change the direction of flight.

To see a *Pteranodon* in flight, you just need some imagination and a pelican! Like pelicans, *Pteranodons* lived by the sea, and flew using slow strokes of their long wings, gliding on air currents when they could. They may even have held their long neck back on their shoulders, and tucked their legs up under their body.

Each flap forces air over the curved wing, creating low pressure above the wing, which generates lift. A delicate change to the angle of the wing alters the amount of lift, and once the bird is moving forward, there may be enough airflow for it to glide. The wing shape is ideal for flapping and gliding, just like an albatross wing.

A long, thin wing like a *Pteranodon's* generates a lot of lift, even when it isn't flapping. Life on a tropical coast means plenty of updraughts, so once airborne, the *Pteranodon* could ride the air currents.

Early theories stated that pterosaurs could not possibly have flown by flapping their wings. They didn't have huge chest muscles like birds, and being cold-blooded they couldn't generate the muscle power of a bat. Surely pterosaurs could only glide, with their thin, delicate wing membranes no more controllable than the average kite.

So how on earth could such a mess have been the top airborne predator for 140 million years? Because the theories were wrong. Firstly, *every* flying animal flaps its wings – master gliders like albatrosses simply flap them less than sparrows do! Secondly, there are cold-blooded flying animals by the billion – bees, butterflies and dragonflies are all spectacular fliers, with special behaviour to warm up their muscles before flight.

Pterosaur skeletons show many adaptations for flight, but recent discoveries have uncovered more of the fine details.

Fragments of pterosaur wing which have been found, clearly show microscopic strengthening fibres running across the wing from the finger bone. These would make the living wing membrane as tough as any plastic sheet.

A Russian fossil of the pterosaur *Sordes pilosus* has signs of hair around the body. This would have helped to keep muscle heat in, and improve flight efficiency – so pterosaurs may have looked like bats, with hairy bodies and fine membranous wings!

The Ocean Reptiles

Swimming is easier than flying, and most reptiles can swim a little, sweeping their tail from side to side like an oar. Animals that live their whole life in the water have to develop much more efficient methods of getting around, and change from walking to swimming by replacing feet with flippers and improving their breath-holding abilities. Turtles have done this, swimming huge distances across the oceans using a gentle rowing motion, and are able to navigate their way to breeding beaches on islands in mid-ocean. One Green turtle was recorded as swimming 1960 km from its breeding grounds in Costa Rica to Mexico in just 275 days!

Plesiosaurs and ichthyosaurs are completely different types of animal, adapted for life in the sea in different ways.

Plesiosaurus

Ophthalamosaurus

The plesiosaur skeleton is very similar to a basic dinosaur pattern, with a long neck and tail, but the limbs are short and square, and the hand bones flattened to form a paddle. The paddles were attached to the shoulders and the pelvic girdle in such a way that they could not be raised above the level of the breast-bone, and could only be flapped up and down, like the wings of a penguin or the flippers of a sea turtle. *Plesiosaurus* had a small head and simple pointed teeth, and hunted by swimming amongst shoals of fish, changing direction using its flippers, and darting its neck out to catch its prey as the shoal broke up. It's likely that it swam around with its head and neck clear of the water, and it may have crawled onto the land to breed, just as turtles do today.

Ichthyosaurs had totally broken contact with the land in favour of life in the sea. The muscular tail had a broad tail fin, and this supplied all the power to push the animal through the water. The flippers and dorsal fin were used for steering. The backbone had hundreds of simple, round vertebrae, for flexibility rather than for supporting the weight of the body, and the skull was a long, toothed beak.

This is the body pattern we last saw in the lungfish, at the start of the story – the ichthyosaurs had returned to the water. Like the plesiosaurs, they fed on fish and squid, and some fossils even contain the remains of pterosaur bones.

The combination of power from the tail and steering from the fins made them very manoeuvrable underwater, and very effective hunters. They hunted visually, and most had large eyes. The Jurassic ichthyosaur *Ophthalamosaurus*, had eyes 19 cm in diameter.

In many ways, ichthyosaurs are similar to dolphins. Both have adapted from land into water, they are effective predators with good sensory systems and perfect streamlining. The only difference is that the ichthyosaurs were swimming around 100 million years before dolphins evolved.

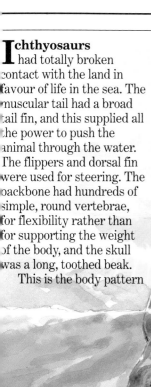

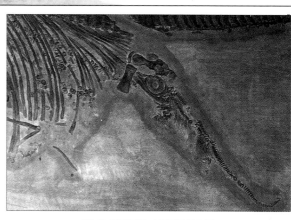

FOSSIL BIRTH

The total commitment to life in the water causes a problem, because reptile eggs can only develop on land. Even today, ocean-going turtles have to return to land to lay their eggs, so how did the ichthyosaurs manage in the sea?

The discovery of this fossil ichthyosaur at Holzmaden in Germany solved the mystery, because it shows an adult female, with a baby emerging from it. Rather than laying an egg, the baby developed inside the mother until it was independent and she gave birth to a live baby, just as dolphins and whales do. This mother seems to have died during the birth, so maybe live birth was risky.

Archaeopteryx–the First Bird

Probably the most extraordinary fossil from the Dinosaur Age was discovered in 1861 in a piece of lithographic limestone at Solnhofen in Germany. This limestone was used in printing because it had such a fine grain, and this was the vital factor in recording a unique type of dinosaur – one with feathers! The skeleton is so similar to that of *Compsognathus* that a later specimen was mis-named, but the feather impressions put it in a new group, and earned it the name *Archaeopteryx* – 'ancient wing'.

What was the first recorded bird really like? It was about the size and shape of a magpie, with a long tail, and wings just like a modern bird's. In the Jurassic period, the Solnhofen area was a salt-water lagoon, with islands inhabited by a variety of wildlife. It's thought that *Archaeopteryx* lived in areas with patchy thickets, feeding on insects and gliding from one bush to the next, safe from predators on the ground.

Since the limestone is only laid down in seawater, it's incredibly lucky that there were both the *Archaeopteryx* and the limestone deposits in the same area. Its skeleton shows a mixture of bird and reptile features.

Teeth–not a feature found in birds today!

Archaeopteryx had a reptilian brain.

The feather layout was similar to that of modern birds, but the bones forming the wings were completely different.

The feathers were shaped for the best airflow, but not anchored in the bones.

The wings had three claws, shaped just like a squirrel's, suggesting that it clambered up trees to find a good launching point.

Typical dinosaur running legs suggest it spent a lot of time on the ground. Its first toe pointed backwards, so that it was able to perch like a bird.

Archaeopteryx had a long, bony tail.

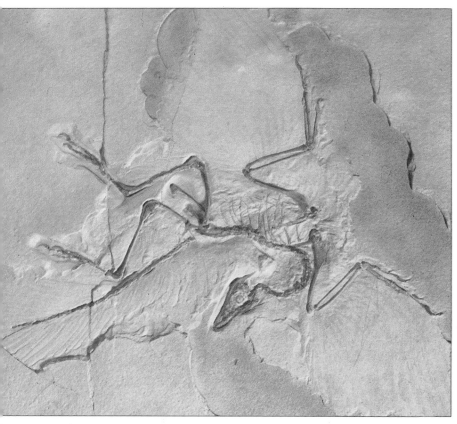

Did *Archaeopteryx* **Fly?** The skeleton does not show the deep chest muscles of modern birds, or the lung system they have developed for active flight, so it's likely that *Archaeopteryx* was a limited aeronaut. But gliding was very useful — living in the pines and tree-ferns would keep it out of the way of the ground predators, and it could clamber up any tree to regain the height it lost on a glide, rather like flying squirrels do today.

How did Birds Evolve?

We are incredibly lucky to have found the fossils of *Archaeopteryx* — and there's a 55-million-year gap before the next clear evidence of bird evolution! Twenty-three species of true birds have been discovered from the Cretaceous period, but only tiny fragments remain of most of them. Only two species of seabirds are well-known: *Ichthyornis* and *Hesperornis*.

Ichthyornis was just like a modern bird, standing about 20 cm high, and shaped like a tern. It had strong flight muscles, a feathered tail anchored to a knob of fused tail-bones, and a pointed beak, probably without teeth.

Hesperornis was a very interesting bird, a diver with stubby wings and feet set well back down the body, acting as paddles. This means it must have given up the power of flight in air! It may have "flown" underwater to catch fish like a penguin.

The Jurassic Earth

Our detective work has taken the dinosaur story a long way from the reconstructed skeleton in the museum, and now we know enough to imagine the environment that the dinosaurs lived in.

In the Jurassic period, from 200 to 135 years ago, the reptiles took over all the Earth's habitats, so how did the Earth look then?

Throughout the period, the huge land mass of Pangaea slowly split up, with lakes and seas flooding low-lying areas. The settled, warm climate of the Triassic changed to a cooler one, with more seasonal changes.

In the damper areas, the land was covered by forests of cycads, tree-ferns and primitive conifer trees like the monkeypuzzle trees today. Their tough leaves, and the softer leaves of ginkgo trees, were the food of the sauropods. In drier areas away from the forests there was patchy scrub, and marshy areas supported ferns and other spore-producing plants.

Lake-shores and rivers like this would probably have been a favourite dinosaur habitat, with plenty of water and vegetation, and sandy soils in which they could lay their eggs.

Pterosaurs ❶
lived around cliffs where
the air currents provided lift to
help them glide,
were plenty of fish to eat.

Sauropods ❷ were the
main plant-eaters, munching
over 100 kilos a day. They
lived in herds, relying on their
huge size to deter predators.
Even their young were safe
from all but the largest
carnivores such as *Allosaurus*.

Stegosaurs ❸ were
another group of large plant-
eaters, found world wide. Like
the sauropods, they died out in
the Cretaceous–except for
some in India, which was then
an island.

The cousins of the
dinosaurs, turtles and
crocodiles ❹ , lived in the
rivers; while dragonflies
❺ hawking along the water's
edge were prey for the small
dinosaurs like *Ornitholestes*,
❻ or even *Archaeopteryx*.

The Cretaceous Earth

The same scene would have looked very different by the late Cretaceous period. The dinosaurs had changed, but the most important difference was the appearance of flowers.

Flowering plants first appeared about 126 million years ago, and by 100 mya they had changed the face of the Earth and set the pattern we see today. Flowering plants included fruit-producing shrubs, vegetables and trees. They had bigger, flatter leaves to absorb as much sunlight as possible, and a complex system to supply water to the leaves, where they manufactured their own food. They produced flowers, then fruits and seeds as part of their life cycle, and the animals adapted to exploit this huge new source of food.

Butterflies and bees became vital plant pollinators, whilst birds, mammals and dinosaurs added fruit and seeds to their diet of leaves.

The continental movements continued, with North America separating from Europe, and the other continents spreading away from the Equator into areas with more seasonal climates.

We know of 23 species of Cretaceous bird, ❶ most of which lived near water, including primitive flamingoes. There were probably thousands more but only those that died in fine silt sediments will have been fossilised.

The ceratopsids ❷ were a very important group, with over 14 different species. They ate plants at ground level, with powerful jaws that could rip up shrubs.

Tyrannosaurus ❸ was the biggest land carnivore ever, a muscular bipedal dinosaur armed with teeth 15 cm long. It may have lived simply by frightening other dinosaurs from their kills.

The hadrosaurs ❹ were also important plant-eaters. Living in herds, communicating by calls and looking after their young, they were sophisticated animals, as tall as houses.

Birds were well established, but mammals ❺ had developed little since the Jurassic period. They were mainly nocturnal and lived in burrows. Now even these were being invaded – by snakes!

The Frilled Dinosaurs

Some of the most impressive dinosaur fossils are the skulls of the ceratopsids, with huge frills at the back of the head and horns at the front. The Ceratopsids were certainly capable of defending themselves and their young from the large predatory dinosaurs of the Cretaceous period. The skull of these huge, rhino-like plant-eaters was formed into a shield of bone and muscle, with horns over a metre long! Provided they could turn to face the predator, they were safe from attack – even the largest carnivores would back down.

The frill was so heavy that the first three neck bones were fused together to act as a support, with the skull balanced on the neck joint like a see-saw.

Weak adults or young animals would have been more vulnerable to attack from behind, where the frill could only help to protect the neck. It's likely that some species such as *Centrosaurus* lived in herds, so the young could be protected from predators inside a defensive ring of adults.

This defensive strength meant that the ceratopsids were very successful animals, with a variety of species found in different habitats. In fact they account for 85 per cent of herbivore fossils from the late Cretaceous period.

Ceratopsids ate at ground level, and moved on all fours. They had a wide, stocky body with a short tail and short legs, but the muscle scars show that the legs were very strong, and much more flexible than a sauropod leg. These herbivores could trot or gallop, just like a modern rhino.

They were able to rip up whole plants using a beak and jaw muscles that attached to the frill. So the frill had two vital functions, in feeding and defence.

Although the Ceratopsids vary in size, they are all the same basic shape, except for the frills. The largest frill is found on *Torosaurus*, as part of a skull over 2.5 metres long, the large skull of any land anim Others have different shapes or horn layout

Centrosaurus, a medium sized, short-frilled type has spines around the edge of the frill, and a single nose horn. But the most obvious features are the two horns that fold down from the top of the frill. These cover openings in the frill, but their function is a mystery. Most ceratopsids had small bony studs around the edge of the frill, but in *Styracosaurus* these formed three long horns on each side.

These may have been used for defence, or for rutting. While the defensive horns point forward, for jabbing at attackers, these horns could lock with another male's, just like the antlers of a deer. Imagine a trial of strength between two snorting male *Styracosaurus*, each weighing about 2 tonnes!

Chasmosaurus is a smaller, long frilled type. Here the frill is so large that the bones only form a frame, with spaces that

would have been filled with muscle and covered by scaly skin. The long frilled species came later than the short frilled

types, so it's likely that once the defensive role of the frill was established, it grew bigger purely for show.

Styracosaurus
Centrosaurus

A living bulldozer?
Triceratops was the largest of the group, standing 3 metres high, 9 metres long, and weighing up to 6 tonnes. Its frill is solid bone, with two long horns just above the eyes for defence. It's thought that this species lived in family groups on open woodland, with the parents protecting their own young, rather than forming defensive rings like the herd dwellers. These animals would eat huge amounts of plant food, ripping up shrubs and branches with the beak, and crushing the leaves with molar teeth at the back of the mouth. The skulls also show huge openings behind the nostrils, so they probably had a good sense of smell, and may have grubbed up roots and tubers using the powerful neck muscles and the beak.

Dinosaurs in Armour

The traditional view of dinosaurs is of slow, lumbering animals armed with claws and covered in scaly armour; but although reptile skin is tough, real bone armour was quite rare amongst dinosaurs, just as it is amongst modern animals. Armour certainly provides protection, but the problem for the animal is of always having to carry it around!

The nodosaurs were the first heavily armoured dinosaurs, appearing in the late Jurassic. They were four-legged ornithischian dinosaurs, with a flat, broad back and horns along their flanks. By the Cretaceous, they had been joined by another group, the ankylosaurs, which browsed on the ground vegetation protected by their massive armour.

Euoplocephalus was one of the largest ankylosaurs, 6 metres long and weighing 2 tonnes. It had plates of bone embedded in its skin, forming studs and nodules, and complete bands of armour across its body: two on the neck, four across the back and three on the hips. This gave it enough flexibility to move around, without leaving chinks in the armour.

Apart from this, *Euoplocephalus* was a primitive dinosaur, a browsing herbivore with simple teeth rather than the plant-grinding tooth batteries of the hadrosaurs. Its skull had a large nasal cavity, which suggests that it had a good sense of smell, useful for grubbing out tubers and roots.

Euoplocephalus (left) could also defend itself by swinging its tail, which had fused bones and ended in two huge lumps of bone, like a club. With a swing of the hips and a flick of the upper tail, this weapon could certainly break the bones of a predator that came too close, so tackling a *Euoplocephalus* meant risking a crippling injury.

If the threat of injury did not deter a predator, then the *Euoplocephalus* (above) would crouch so all the softer parts of its body were protected behind the armour. The bands stretched down the sides to form a skirt, and by tucking in its legs and digging in with its strong claws, there was no way for a predator to wound the ankylosaur. Bony plates covering the skull gave the animal's head additional protection. *Euoplocephalus* even had armoured eyelids to protect its eyes from predators' claws.

Euoplocephalus

Armadillos (like the one above) and pangolins are among the few modern animals to have armour. It is formed from bony plates and thickened skin, appearing rather like fingernails. This makes it quite light, so they are active animals and only use their defensive armour when cornered. Then they roll up to protect their soft stomach, presenting predators with a tough ball that's impossible to prise open. Armadillo armour is split into a lot of bands so they can roll up tight, and pangolins may have over 1000 scales, as spiky as a pineapple.

What was the Fastest Dinosaur

In the Cretaceous period, the smaller dinosaurs and plant-eaters needed defences against the carnivores – horns, armour, or simple speed.

The fastest dinosaur was also the fastest animal on Earth, almost certainly an ornithomimosaur, a dinosaur that ran on two legs but at twice the speed of a human sprinter!

The ornithomimosaurs were theropods, a group that started with *Coelophysis*, and they were athletes. They had long legs with long toes for extra power, a backbone stiffened at the pelvis to support the leg muscles, and claws flattened like running spikes. The head and tail were small and light, with the tailbones stiffened for use as a rudder to help balance.

Struthiomimus was one of the largest of the group, standing about 2 metres tall, and 4 metres from head to tail.

Its skull has large eyes, and is light and flexible. It probably ate insects, fruit and seeds, and used its speed for escape rather than for hunting.

Its skeleton is incredibly similar to that of an ostrich, except that it has the bonus of long arms with three clawed fingers that could form a proper hand. This would be useful for catching insects or grasping plants, or holding food up to the beak.

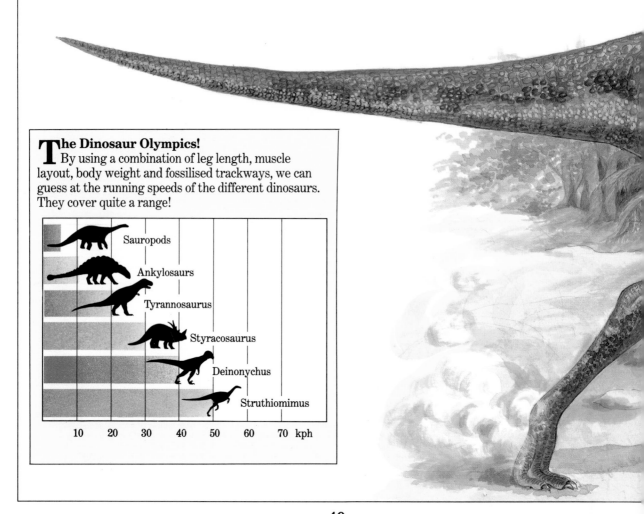

The Dinosaur Olympics!

By using a combination of leg length, muscle layout, body weight and fossilised trackways, we can guess at the running speeds of the different dinosaurs. They cover quite a range!

Sauropods

Ankylosaurs

Tyrannosaurus

Styracosaurus

Deinonychus

Struthiomimus

10   20   30   40   50   60   70   kph

Struthio vs Struthiomimus

S The skeleton of the ostrich (*Struthio*) is similar in almost every respect, so it's reasonable to imagine *Struthiomimus* as a large ostrich, with a scaly skin, arms and a tail. Both have a beak rather than teeth, and rely on a gizzard to break down their food. Ostriches are renowned for their ability to eat almost anything!

Which was the Most Dangerou

Tyrannosaurus (left) stood over 5 metres tall, with a mouth a metre long. Could such a huge animal move quickly? Just how dangerous was it?

It had tiny, two-clawed forelimbs that could barely reach its mouth, and it couldn't stand on one leg and strike with the other, so those mighty jaws were its only weapon. It may have ambushed its prey, running at it with jaws wide open and catching it by the neck in one tremendous bite.

But how would a predator the size of a hous manage to hide itself? Maybe it didn't bother, bu walked around the Cretaceous woodlands frightening other dinosau from their prey. Certainly no other dinosaur would attack a *Tyrannosaurus*, and eating would be easy. One huge clawed foot would hold the body down whilst the jaws ripped up chunks of flesh – without the need of forelimbs.

This is exactly how vultures feed – but more c them later.

A single *Deinonychus* would attack smaller dinosaurs up to the size of a hypsilophodont, like this one. It could stalk or ambush, hiding amongst vegetation and selecting a target before attacking, then using its speed to run down its prey.

It's likely that they also hunted in packs, like lions do today, because this is much easier. The group can take larger prey by attacking from all sides. By sharing out the meat, they dispose of the kill faster, without attracting the attention of other predators. Five *Deinonychus* skeletons have been found around one *Tenetosaurus* (a Cretaceous sauropod), so maybe they sometimes came off worst in a fight!

Deinonychus

Tyrannosaurus

The undoubted lords of the Cretaceous period were the carnivorous inosaurs, but which were the most ffective hunters, the most dangerous inosaurs? Really dangerous animals are oth fast and well-armed, so tooth size nd shape, claw size, jaw strength and leg ength are all important clues in our hunt.

Deinonychus (below) was a classic unting dinosaur. It stood about the same eight as a man, but had a large head with 0 sharp teeth, and powerful jaw muscles. ts forelimbs were long and strong, with 3 rasping claws, but its main weapon was a long claw on the second toe of its foot.

Deinonychus was certainly a fast dinosaur, and it probably ran after its prey, holding the long claw off the ground. It grabbed with its forelimbs to pull the quarry down, then killed by biting and kicking, flicking the large claw at the end of the kick to slash through the flesh. Its tail was strengthened with rods, so it may have leant back on it to keep its balance whilst it stood on one leg and kicked with the other. Modern-day male kangaroos box like this – but imagine one with a 10 cm claw on each foot!

The Challenger

Recent discoveries claim the largest carnivorous dinosaur was not *Tyrannosaurus*, but a Jurassic carnosaur called *Epanterias*. It weighed about four tonnes, was almost ten metres long and combined the jaws of *Tyrannosaurus* with powerful clawed forelimbs. Bones from only three skeletons have been found, but this may have been the most dangerous of them all!

Did Dinosaurs make Noises?

If all we have left from the dinosaur age are bones and footprints, how can we tell if dinosaurs made noises? By looking *inside* the skulls!

The hadrosaurs were one of the most successful plant-eating groups of the Cretaceous period, with over twenty different species. They had very efficient teeth, but these were designed for plant-crushing, not combat. Most hadrosaur skulls also have a hollow crest rising from the forehead, in a variety of different shapes, and this is thought to have been a sound generator.

The skull cavity of one hadrosaur, *Lambeosaurus*, has been modelled on a computer and linked to a synthesiser. Fed with data about dinosaur lung output and the dimensions of the skull chamber, it produced a loud, trumpeting call.

The skull of *Corythosaurus*, another crested hadrosaur, contains the very fine bones that transmit sound within the ear, showing that hadrosaur hearing was good as well.

It seems likely that the different crests produced different sounds, but sound production is very rare amongst modern reptiles, so why should hadrosaurs make noises? The simple answer is defence. Hadrosaurs were big animals, between seven and ten metres long, but they fed head down in herds with their young, so they were very vulnerable to surprise attack. So if some of the herd acted as guards, they would be safe – but only if the guards were able to raise the alarm by making a call!

Parasaurolophus (far right) had the largest crest, up to 1.8 metres long and stretching back over the head. A pair of tubes from the nose to the throat doubled back inside the crest like a trombone.

Parasaurolophus ate ground-level plants, reaching forward to bite, then using its tail as a counterbalance to stand upright while it chewed. Because the crest tubes are attached to the nostrils, it could chew and call at the same time.

Geese face the same problems, and a feeding flock will always include some look-outs who will honk very loudly if there is danger – in fact, they're renowned as "watch dogs".

Corythosaurus (below) had a large, plate-like crest that may also have been coloured to act as a visual signal as well as a sound organ.

Saurolophus (above) had a spike at the back of its skull which may have supported a fleshy bag on the top of the snout. The bag was blown up to make a noise like air escaping from a balloon.

Tsintaosaurus (left) had a simple hollow tube that jutted out of the forehead, with two bulbs at the base.

Baby Dinosaurs

In 1978, in Montana in the USA, scientist John Horner discovered the first of a whole series of complete dinosaur nests! Like most reptiles, dinosaurs laid large clutches of eggs into nests scraped out of sand, and careful analysis of the eggs and even the babies inside them shows that some dinosaurs looked after their young, just like the birds in your garden.

Horner found nesting colonies of two very different dinosaurs. One colony belonged to *Maiasaura*, a hadrosaur, but there were also nests of *Orodromeus*, a smaller plant-eating hypsilophodont dinosaur.

The hypsilophodont babies left the nest immediately after hatching to follow their parents to feeding grounds, but some of the young *Maiasaura* lived on the nest for months after hatching and were fed by their parents.

This model is based on a computer scan inside a hypsilophodont egg, 75 million years after it was laid! The pointed shape fits a large baby in a small egg, so newly hatched hypsilophodonts were big and very well-developed.

The *Maiasaura* nest (opposite) was carefully built, with a cup about 2 metres across, probably scraped up by the adult as she sat on the top – a technique used by flamingoes today. The nests were positioned two neck-lengths apart, in a large communal rookery, and the mothers may have covered the eggs with rotting vegetation to help incubation.

The rounded, 20 cm eggs hatched into young hadrosaurs about 35 cm from head to tail – one hundredth the size of their parents. Because the young were so small, the females could lay smaller eggs, and more of them. They stayed on the nest until they were about a metre long, then joined the family herd, growing steadily to reach 3 metres long by their first birthday.

The communal nature of the hadrosaurs meant the colony was well defended.

Hypsilophodont eggs (right) were arranged in spirals, partially buried in warm sand. The eggs are about 17 cm long and pointed, and the number of broken shells and lack of baby skeletons is evidence that the babies could walk when very young, and left the nest.

Modern ground-nesting birds like pheasants can do the same – a vital way of protecting the young from predators.

Adult *Maiasaura*

Maiasaura hatchling

How Stupid were Dinosaurs?

If something is clumsy, out-sized or old-fashioned, we call it a "dinosaur", whether it's a car or a rock band! Yet the likes of *Deinonychus*, *Struthiomimus* or *Maiasaura* were amazing animals – fast, agile, alert and communicative, and a long way from the standard image we have today of the lumbering dinosaur.

The final insult for dinosaurs is that they had tiny brains and were stupid – but how true is that?

Measuring intelligence in living animals is very difficult, and the fossil record isn't much help, because the only evidence is the size of the cavity that once held the brain! In mammals and birds, this is about the same size as the brain itself, but in reptiles the brain often fills only half the cavity.

Comparing probable brain size with body size shows which animals had the largest brain in proportion to their body, and at either end of the dinosaur range are *Stegosaurus* and *Stenonychosaurus*.

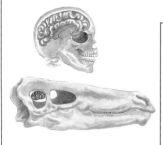

The reptile brain

is a long smooth tube, with nerves running from it. It is quite unlike a human brain, which appears wrinkled and has huge lobes on top of the smooth part. An "intelligent" brain must have a large surface area and well-developed lobes for processing information from the senses. The surface of the human brain is so folded that it has a huge surface area making us the most intelligent, successful animals on Earth.

Stegosaurus

weighed about 1.5 tonnes, but had a brain weighing just 70 g. This is a tiny brain – a 1.5-tonne elephant would have a brain thirty times bigger! *Stegosaurus* lived in the Jurassic period. It was a plant-eater, with a small head and simple teeth, and may have needed gizzard stones like the sauropods in order to digest its food. Its hind legs were longer than its forelegs, and it is often shown in a sprawling pose, though it could probably have stood on its hind legs to reach higher shoots, and may have been able to move on two legs or on four, just like an *Iguanodon*.

The plates on its back were once thought to have been for defence, but they have a rich supply of blood vessels and are exactly the right shape to act as radiators, helping the *Stegosaurus* to warm up in the cold mornings and keep cool in the heat of the day. So the image of *Stegosaurus* is of an untroubled animal, grazing its way through life – and a 70 g brain is quite suitable.

Stenonychosaurus
The largest dinosaur brains are found among the bipedal hunting dinosaurs, with good senses of vision and balance.

Stenonychosaurus had a brain larger than that of a modern reptile, and very similar to a bird's brain with lobes for vision and smell filling the skull cavity.

Stenonychosaurus was a small bipedal predator from the late Cretaceous. It stood about a metre tall, and had eyes arranged for stereo vision. Its forelimbs were long and ended in grasping claws, so it would have had good co-ordination between its eyes and hands, just as we do. It probably hunted the mammals that appeared around dusk, and must have been able to move fast to catch them.

So there were dinosaurs with the brain power of modern animals, which hunted by judging distances, predicting the movement of very agile prey, and outwitting the mammals. We've also found evidence of dinosaur communication and parental care, so it's obvious that some dinosaurs were very special animals, as sophisticated as any alive today, and their extinction was a catastrophe.

Stegosaurus

Stenonychosaurus

The End of the Dinosaurs

Imagine a warm summer's day in the late Cretaceous period about 64 million years ago. The air is busy with insects, buzzing around the dinosaurs that are grazing the flowers and shrubs. Ankylosaurs and ceratopsids plod around, protected by their weaponry. A noisy group of hadrosaurs call as they feed, and ornithomimosaurs strut around, running a few paces to stay clear of danger.

Roving packs of smaller hunters follow the hypsilophodonts, looking for the weakling that provides a meal, and everything gives a *Tyrannosaurus* a wide berth!

On land, the dinosaurs have a balance between hunter and hunted. There are enormous pterosaurs soaring overhead, a constant buzz of insects, and chattering birds, feasting on the seeds, berries and even catching fish.

The most intriguing theory is that the Earth was hit by a huge meteorite (left). Rocks dated at 64 mya often show a thin band of the element Iridium, which is very rare on Earth, but is found in meteorites. The impact of a huge meteorite, maybe 10 kilometres across, would have shaken the Earth, and produced clouds of Iridium-rich dust that blotted out the Sun, then slowly settled to earth as a thin layer.

The dust would have affected burrowing animals, freshwater animals and small marine creatures least, whilst plants could survive buried in the dust as seeds – but there would be no leaves for the large plant-eating dinosaurs.

A similar dust cloud could be formed by volcanoes (right). The movement of the continents may have weakened the Earth's thin crust enough for millions of tonnes of molten lava to explode into the atmosphere and blot out the Sun.

Or maybe a large meteor broke through the crust, releasing the lava and masses of iridium dust?

The boundaries of the geological periods are marked by changes in the climate and vegetation (above), so it may have been a gradual change that killed off the dinosaurs. Flooding and drought can affect whole populations.

Then, after 140 million years, the Dinosaur Age was over. It certainly didn't end overnight (the process may have taken thousands of years) but the Earth changed dramatically. The change wiped out microscopic plankton and plesiosaurs in the seas, pterosaurs, and any land animal weighing over about 25 kilos – and there were plenty of those! Over 70 per cent of species became extinct, leaving only the warm blooded animals, nocturnal mammals and freshwater species cushioned from the calamity. Only these adaptable animals survived, so what happened? It was certainly something big, and it probably involved blocking out the sunlight that plants, and ultimately animals depend on.

It was a global effect – not due to egg-eating mammals or an increase in dinosaur predators – and it made life so difficult for the dinosaurs that they did not produce enough young to survive, and died out *en masse*.

The Mammals Take Over

Zalambdalestes **was a** typical late Cretaceous mammal. About the size of a large mouse, it was a nocturnal insect-eater, with good eyesight and hearing.

Ninety-five per cent of known mammals appeared after the Cretaceous. *Coryphodon* was a Palaeocene mammal. Over 2 metres long, it looked like a pygmy hippo, with long canine tusks, and it may have lived in rivers and swamps.

Surprisingly, bats like *Icaronycteris* were flying in the early Eocene (50 mya)! It was a fast-flying hunter that took insects on the wing. Its skeleton was like a modern bat's, but with more teeth, a wider wing and a long tail.

Monkeys first appeared 40 million years ago. *Branisella* is the earliest known South American monkey, with a long tail. It appeared about 32 mya.

The Eocene period saw mammals invade the sea and take to the air. *Basilosaurus* was one of the first whales. It was 25 metres long, but slender, with sharp spiky teeth and tail flukes, like those of a modern whale.

135 mya

64 mya

CRETACEOUS
Dinosaurs & Zalambalestes

For almost 140 million years, the dinosaurs had been the top predators on Earth, feeding on everything from insects to each other! In that time they had evolved into specialists, and were unable to cope with the event that ended the Cretaceous.

The opposite was true of mammals: they were small, active, furred animals that controlled their own body temperature and could live almost anywhere. They ate small amounts of seeds and insects, which were still plentiful. The food eaten by one dinosaur would feed 10 000 mammals.

Mammals carry their young protected inside the mother until they are developed, and look after them once they are born, improving their chance of survival. Small mammals don't live very long, but they do breed frequently. So once conditions improved, populations could grow very fast. Animals that breed quickly can adapt to changes in their environment – something that the slow-growing, long-lived dinosaurs simply couldn't do.

In the Miocene (26–7mya), seas covered much of Europe, and *Cetotherium* swam in them. It was a plankton-eating baleen whale like modern species, but just 4 metres long.

Mammuthus trogontherii was a British mammal from the Pleistocene. It was covered in thick hair, stood 4.5 metres high, and fed on the grasses that had replaced much of the world's forest since the Dinosaur Age.

The first elephants appeared in the Miocene. *Gomphotherium* had four tusks – a pair on each jaw. As the species evolved, the trunk formed from the upper lip, growing longer and more useful for feeding. Elephants, hippos and rhinos are all quite common in prehistory.

In the Pliocene (7–2 mya), there were huge camels in North America! *Titanotylophus* was one of the biggest, standing 3.5 metres at the shoulder. It was just like a modern type, but didn't live in a desert, so it didn't have a big hump.

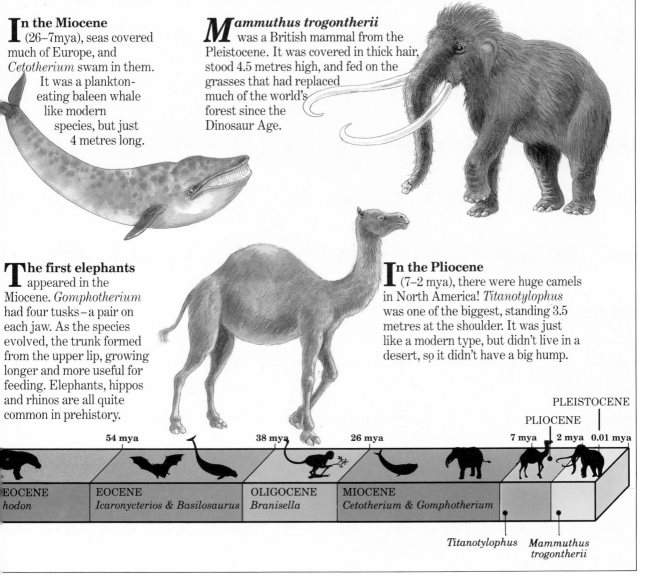

PLEISTOCENE
PLIOCENE

| 54 mya | | 38 mya | 26 mya | | 7 mya | 2 mya | 0.01 mya |

| EOCENE | EOCENE | OLIGOCENE | MIOCENE | | | |
| *hodon* | *Icaronycterios & Basilosaurus* | *Branisella* | *Cetotherium & Gomphotherium* | | | |

Titanotylophus   *Mammuthus trogontherii*

Monster Mammals

We know from fossils that, in the 64 million years since the end of the Cretaceous period, a huge number of mammals have come in to existence and then disappeared. These changes don't happen overnight, but slowly. A population declines until the birth rate cannot match the death rate, and then the animal slips into extinction.

In the modern world, it's generally Man that's to blame, but there have always been "endangered species". Before Man, animal populations increased when conditions were right for them – when the climate suited them, or there was plenty of the right type of plant or prey species. But being too dependent on one food source or habitat can lead to extinction if that food source or habitat is destroyed – and as we've seen, the Earth has been changing throughout its history! So just as *Deinonychus*, *Pteranodon*, *Maiasaura* and all the other dinosaurs became extinct, so also have some fascinating mammals from the age that followed after the dinosaurs.

The largest carnivorous land mammal ever was *Megistotherium* (left), a member of a now extinct family called creodonts. It lived in North Africa during the Miocene period, over 20 million years ago, and weighed up to 900 kg.

It walked flat-footed, and had a small brain and unspecialised teeth, so it was probably a general scavenger rather than a pure hunter. It was quite bear-like, but had a long tail.

The creodonts were the main carnivores in the Eocene period, but they began to be replaced by the true carnivores – cats and dogs – about 35 million years ago.

Rhinoceroses appeared quite early in the mammal expansion, and came in many forms. *Paracerathium* was the largest, standing over 5 metres to the shoulder, and probably weighing about 30 tonnes. It had no horn, and had slightly longer legs than modern rhinos; but like the black rhino of today, it had a long upper lip for pulling at vegetation–in this case, trees over 7 metres off the ground! It lived in Asia around the Pliocene period, when huge areas of dense forest had been replaced by open woodland and grass–an ideal habitat for the mega-rhino.

The cats took over from the creodonts thanks to a larger brain, better senses and long limbs, which made them fast enough to catch any herbivore. This large, muscular cat (below) known as *Smilodon* is one of the most famous extinct mammals. It lived in America from the late Pliocene into the Pleistocene, and was a very effective predator, with claws that it could sheath when running and a pair of huge teeth on its upper jaw. It probably killed by jumping at its prey, holding on with its claws and by stabbing with the teeth. *Smilodon* has been found at one of the world's best fossil sites, the La Brea Tar Pits in Los Angeles. In the Pleistocene, the pit was covered by shallow water, and looked just like a lake, but animals coming to drink were trapped by the tar and died–perfectly preserved for modern-day fossil-hunters!

The Appearance of Man

The Earth is now dominated by one mammal–Man. No dinosaur had such an effect on the environment as we have had, and we've been around less than 0.1 million years, not 120 million!

Trying to trace the history of one species from the patchy fossil record is very difficult, but there has been a steady development of human-type fossils through the ages, with increasing brain size, a flatter face and more mobile hands.

The story starts 4 million years ago, with an "ape-man" *Australopithecus*, which stood upright, about 1.4 metres tall. It lived in grassy African savannah, and had a very ape-like skull, with a brain just one-third the size of modern Man's brain.

The Cro-Magnons were very effective hunters, and paintings like this one from France (below) depict the hunt. The paintings show they had spare time, and that recording the hunts was important in their society, as a sign of strength, or even the beginnings of a religion.

The Cro-Magnons made their tools carefully, chipping at flints to form sharp spear points and knives.

The population explosion. At the time of *Homo sapiens* the world population of humans was about 10 million, but man has increased his control over the enviroment to allow for a larger population to grow.

The human population growth rate is getting faster. By the end of this century, there may be 6 billion people on Earth!

population in billions

5.7
4
2

0 000   8 000   6 000   4 000   2 000   BC AD 500   1 000   1 500   2 000

The first remains of true Man, *Homo habilis*, are just under 2 million years old. *Homo habilis* had a flatter, more human face, and feet and hands just like ours, so he could have made stone tools.

Three hundred thousand years later the remains of *Homo erectus*, a more advanced Man with a larger body and brain, start to appear in Europe and Asia as well as Africa.

Our species, *Homo sapiens*, probably first appeared in Africa, maybe 100 000 years ago. The best fossil evidence is of a European type called Cro-Magnon man, dating from about 40 000 years ago. These people lived in groups, in caves or in tents built from animal skins. They hunted in groups, catching deer or wild ox using arrows and spears tipped with sharpened flints or bones. They fished, using hooks and harpoons, set traps for smaller animals, and probably ate wild berries and roots too.

The climate in Europe was similar to the one we have today, so they needed clothing to keep them warm. They made garments from animal skins cut up with stone knives which they sewed together with leather thongs.

At the same time as they spread into Europe, *Homo sapiens* invaded Asia and crossed a land bridge into North America, eventually settling in all the continents of the world.

Are any Dinosaurs Alive Today

The dinosaurs were certainly a very special group of animals, not just lumbering monsters but active, agile and even intelligent!

Whatever it was, and however long it took, the event that ended the Cretaceous certainly wiped out larger dinosaurs like *Triceratops* and *Tyrannosaurus*, but 60 million years earlier a small bi-pedal dinosaur had given rise to *Archaeopteryx*. So the survivors of the dinosaur line were the birds, and they are the dinosaurs that are still alive today!

For a small animal, the ability to fly is a wonderful protection against ground predators, an easy way to travel long distances or spot food. It was a natural development for the fast running dinosaurs, and as you can see on this page, birds are still very similar to their dinosaur ancestors.

So try to imagine the birds running across your lawn scaled up to dinosaur size, with arms and claws instead of wings scales instead of feathers and a reptile tail. You'll be back in the Dinosaur Age!

All birds we have today stand upright on two legs, and many run or walk rather than hopping. This White Backed Vulture feeds just like a tyrannosaur, holding down its meat with a clawed foot and ripping it up by pulling with its mouth. Instead of 70 curved teeth, it has one very strong curved beak.

There were crocodiles in the Dinosaur Age, but they aren't dinosaurs! They arose from the same ancient line as the dinosaurs, and are amongst the oldest types of reptile still found in the world today.

Saltwater crocodiles are the biggest at 4.5 metres long and over 500 kg in weight. They haven't changed in 200 million years because they dominate the tropical rivers and lakes where they live, reigning supreme as top carnivores, just like their dinosaur cousins on land.

Just like *Maiasaura*, flamingoes (left) nest beside lakes and lagoons, in colonies that may number 30 000 nests in Lesser Flamingoes. Each nest is a simple cone of mud scraped up by the parents, and spaced apart from the neighbours. Instead of a huge dinosaur clutch, they lay a simple egg, and feed the chick on a diet of liquid shrimps, dripped from beak to beak.

The other ancient reptile group are the tortoises and turtles (right). Most species are plant eaters, relying on their shell for protection, but the giant land tortoises of Aldabra and the Galapagos only survived because there were no mammal predators on the islands, and were decimated when they were introduced by Man.

Flightless birds like this cassowary (above) are the nearest living equivalent to the bipedal hunting dinosaurs. Cassowaries live in Australia, and are quite dangerous, attacking with kicks from their strong, sharp-clawed hind legs. The head has a bony crest, and bright red and blue skin – just like a dinosaur!

Most film versions of the dinosaur story have animals the size of houses noisily wrestling each other to the ground in a cloud of dust, with snapping jaws and flailing reptile tails.

Would a *Tyrannosaurus* jump on the back of a sauropod and try to kill it? Not likely! Hunting animals take calculated risks every time they try to kill, and they certainly don't select the biggest, strongest opponent.

By looking at both the fossil evidence – bones, teeth, eggs and footprints – and the biology of modern animals, we can see how dinosaurs actually lived. Most eat plants – everthing from small shrubs and roots to whole trees, and many were big enough or organised enough to be safe from attack. Scientists working on fossil skeletons now know a lot about their engineering and the physics of animal movement, and studies of modern animals show how they naturally organise their feeding, their breeding or their family groups.

The great thing about dinosaurs is that anyone can have a theory about how they lived, so long as it isn't opposed by the little hard evidence that exists. What's yours?

Re-building a dinosaur skeleton requires skill and imagination. When the foot of this *Deinonychus* was re-built, the bones showed that the big claw could be held upright, or flicked downwards. It became a weapon, and *Deinonychus* gained a fearsome reputation as a very dangerous hunter.

Animals move in lots of different ways. They walk on two legs or four, they trot, run, canter or gallop, and each of these leaves a different type of track. Dinosaurs have left a lot of tracks, and by carefully analysing the gaps between them, we can discover how they moved.

Dinosaur eggs are relatively common. They are large, their shells fossilise quite easily, and they were often buried in sand. The size of the egg tells us the size of the hatchlings, and their skeletons tell us about the family life of the species. It's even possible to scan a dinosaur egg and see the baby inside!

magine Them?

Masters of a model landscape! They may ok like Triceratops and yrannosaurus, but few m dinosaurs behave like e real thing!

WARNER BROS. Pictures presents

'The Animal World'

Written, Produced and Directed by IRWIN ALLEN
A WINDSOR PRODUC

Colour by TECHNICOLOR

Most dinosaur remains are fragments, so complete skeletons are incredibly valuable. We know a lot about the lifestyle of this ornithomimosaur simply because its skeleton is so similar to an ostriche's! It must have walked bipedally, it must have been able to run fast, and it must have eaten small items of food probably plant and animal, just like modern ostriches do!

Having Trouble with the Names?

All animals have a scientific name which is basically a Latin description of the animal, given by the person who discovered it. Many dinosaur names are long and difficult to say, and some are quite funny, for example, Procompsognathus means "before pretty jaw" Here's some help with pronouncing the names of the dinosaurs and some of the other difficult names in this book.

Allosaurus	Al-lo-saw-rus
Ankylosaur	Ann-kie-low-saw
Apatosaurus	Ap-at-oh-saw-rus
Archaeopteryx	Ark-ee-opt-er-ix
Australopithecus	Ost-ral-oh-pith-ee-kus
Basilosaurus	Baz-ill-oh-saw-rus
Brachiosaurus	Brak-ee-oh-saw-rus
Branisella	Bran-ee-sell-a
Centrosaurus	Sent-ro-saw-rus
Cetotherium	Seat-oh-thee-ree-um
Chasmosaurus	Kaz-mo-saw-rus
Coelophysis	Seal-oh-fie-sis
Compsognathus	Komp-sow-nay-thus
Coryphodon	Core-riff-foe-don
Corythosaurus	Core-ith-oh-saw-rus
Cretaceous	Kret-ay-shus
Cycads	Sigh-kads
Deinonychus	Die-no-nike-us
Diplodocus	Dip-lod-oh-cus
Eocene	Ee-oh-seen
Epanterias	Epp-ant-air-ee-as
Euoplocephalus	You-oh-plo-keff-a-lus
Euparkeria	You-park-ear-ee-a
Gomphotherium	Gomm-foe-thee-ree-um
Gondwana	Gone-dwa-na
Herrarasaurus	Hair-are-rah-saw-rus
Hesperornis	Hess-per-or-niss
Hypsilophodont	Hip-see-low-foe-dont
Icaronycteris	Ik-are-oh-nick-ter-iss
Ichthyornis	Ik-thee-or-niss
Ichthyostega	Ik-thee-oh-stee-ga
Ichthyosaur	Ik-thee-oh-saw
Iguanodon	Ig-wa-no-don
Jurassic	Jew-rah-sic

Lambeosaurus	Lamb-bee-oh-saw-rus
Lesothosaurus	Less-oh-tho-saw-rus
Maiasaura	My-ah-saw-rah
Mamenchisaurus	Mam-enk-ee-saw-rus
Mammuthus trogontherii	Mam-oo-thus trow-gonth-ear-ee-eye
Megistotherium	Me-jist-oh-theer-ee-um
Miocene	My-oh-seen
Oligocene	Oll-ee-go-seen
Ophthalamosaurus	Off-thal-ammo-saw-rus
Ornithischian	Or-nith-ish-she-an
Ornitholestes	Or-nith-oh-less-teez
Orodromeus	Or-ro-dro-me-us
Oviraptor	Oh-vee-rap-tor
Palaeocene	Pal-ee-oh-seen
Pangaea	Pan-gay-a
Paraceratherium	Para-sarah-theer-ee-um
Parasaurolophus	Para-saw-ro-low-fuss
Plateosaurus	Platt-ee-o-saw-rus
Pleistocene	Ply-stow-seen
Plesiosaur	Plez-ee-oh-saw
Pliocene	Ply-oh-seen
Pliosaur	Ply-oh-saw
Protoceratops	Pro-toe-sarah-tops
Pterosaur	Terro-saw
Quetzalcoatylus	Kwet-zal-co-at-ee-lus
Rhamphorhyncus	Ram-foe-rink-us
Saurischian	Saw-rish-she-an
Saurolophus	Saw-ro-low-fuss
Seismosaurus	Size-mo-saw-rus
Smilodon	Smile-oh-don
Sordes pliosus	Saw-dez pill-oh-sus
Staurikosaurus	Store-rick-o-saw-rus
Stenonychosaurus	Sten-oh-nike-oh-saw-rus
Stegosaurus	Steg-oh-saw-rus
Struthiomimus	Strew-thee-oh-mime-us
Styracosaurus	Sty-rack-oh-saw-rus
Titanotylophus	Tie-tan-oh-tie-low-fuss
Torosaurus	Tor-ro-saw-rus
Triassic	Try-ass-ic
Triceratops	Try-se-rah-tops
Tsintaosaurus	Sint-ow-saw-rus
Tyrannosaurus	Tie-ran-no-saw-rus
Zalambalestes	Zal-am-bar-less-teez

Index